HAPPY BIRTHDAY ANDREW

THOUGHT THIS LITTLE BOOK.
WOULD MAKE YOU . SMILE!!

ISABEL x

You're
NOT OLD
YOU'RE JUST
NOT THAT YOUNG

YOU'RE NOT OLD, YOU'RE JUST NOT THAT YOUNG

This expanded and revised edition © Summersdale Publishers Ltd, 2018

First published in 2012

With new text by Chris Stone

An Hachette UK Company
www.hachette.co.uk

Summersdale Publishers Ltd
Part of Octopus Publishing Group Limited
Carmelite House
50 Victoria Embankment
LONDON
EC4Y 0DZ

www.summersdale.com

Printed and bound in Poland

ISBN: 978-1-78685-055-3

Substantial discounts on bulk quantities of Summersdale books are available to corporations, professional associations and other organisations. For details contact general enquiries: telephone: +44 (0) 1243 771107 or email: enquiries@summersdale.com.

You're NOT OLD

YOU'RE JUST NOT THAT YOUNG

HARVEY LITTLE

summersdale

To..

From..

CONTENTS

....

THE BRIGHT SIDE

First you are young; then you are middle-aged; then you are old; then you are wonderful.

Lady Diana Cooper

Whatever with the past has gone, the best is always yet to come.

LUCY LARCOM

I'm happy to report that my inner child is still ageless.

James Broughton

....

A newspaper reporter is sent to interview a local woman who has reached the remarkable age of 109. He asks her various questions, including the secret of her longevity, and finishes off by asking: 'And what do you think is the best thing about being 109?' 'No peer pressure,' she deadpans.

....

Youth is the gift of nature, but age is a work of art.

Garson Kanin

Three old-timers, aged 70, 80 and 90, are talking about the stresses and strains of old age. The conversation soon turns to their morning bowel movements.

'I wake up every morning at seven sharp,' says the youngest man, 'and it takes me at least fifteen minutes to wee.'

'I'm even worse than that,' says the next man. 'I rise at eight and I sit there for forty-five minutes before I can get anything out.'

The oldest of the three then says, 'Well at seven I pee like a horse and at eight I crap like a cow.'

His two friends are really taken aback. 'What's the problem then?' they ask.

'I don't wake up until nine.'

Just remember, once you're over the hill,
you begin to pick up speed.

Charles M. Schulz

....

I can still rock like a son of a b*tch.

Ozzy Osbourne

....

To be 70 years young is sometimes
far more cheerful and hopeful
than to be 40 years old.

Oliver Wendell Holmes Jr

Proof that you can do what you love well into old age is Adam Kelly, Britain's oldest ice-cream man. He retired in 2016 at the grand age of 95, after doing what he did six days of the week, every week – selling ice cream!

An elderly man discovers he doesn't have long to live. He summons his doctor, his priest and his lawyer to tell them the news. 'I need to ask you three a favour before I die,' he says. 'I'm going to give each of you fifty thousand pounds in cash. When I die, I want all three of you to throw the money in my grave.'

A few days later the old man passes away. After the funeral the three men meet up. The doctor says, 'I've got to admit – I kept twenty per cent of his money, but he did owe me a lot in medical bills. I threw the other forty thousand in.'

The priest says, 'I have a confession too. I donated half his money to the church, but I threw the other twenty-five thousand in'.

The lawyer can't believe his ears. 'Well, I'm surprised at you two,' he says. 'I wrote a cheque for the whole amount and threw it in.'

Our wrinkles are our medals of the passage of life. They are what we have been through...

Lauren Hutton

....

As he heads into the pub a middle-aged man spots a bewildered old soul appearing to fish in a puddle outside. Taking pity, he offers to buy him a drink. As they sip their whiskeys, the younger man decides to lighten the mood and asks, 'So, how many have you caught today?' The old man replies, 'Oh, you're the ninth.'

....

A comfortable old age is the reward of a well-spent youth.

Maurice Chevalier

I am getting to an age when I can only enjoy the last sport left. It is called hunting for your spectacles.

EDWARD GREY

Autumn is really the best of the seasons; and I'm not sure that old age isn't the best part of life.

C. S. Lewis

....

A septuagenarian couple are reviewing
the architect's plans for the building of their
new home. The contractor is concerned by the
atrium window for the walk-in shower.
'I'm worried your neighbours will have the perfect
view of you au naturel,' he says to the man.
'Don't worry,' says the man's wife.
'They'll only look once.'

....

You only live once, but if you do it right, once is enough.

Mae West

Little old ladies Edith and Olive are out driving.
Both of them can barely see over the dashboard.
When they reach a set of traffic lights they drive straight
through, accompanied by lots of beeping horns.
Edith, in the passenger seat, thinks, 'I must be going crazy.
I could have sworn we just went through a red light.'
A few minutes later, another set of lights and the same
thing happens again – and again she questions herself.
So Edith starts paying really close attention.
Sure enough, at the next junction the light is
definitely red and they run right through it.
She exclaims to her friend, 'God, Olive! Do you realise
we just ran through three red lights in a row?
You could have killed us!'
Olive turns to her and says, 'Oh, am I driving?'

Youth is for freedom and reform, maturity for judicious compromise, and old age for stability and repose.

Winston Churchill

....

Sixty-year-old Jan is discussing her new
college course with her husband, Yosef.
She's a very mature student and, not surprisingly,
by far the oldest in the class.
'Even the teacher is younger than I am,' she moans.
'Well I think it's great,' says Yosef. 'I thought my
days of fooling around with college girls were over.'

....

Old age likes indecency. It's a sign of life.

Mason Cooley

Men are like wine. Some turn to vinegar, but the best improve with age.

Pope John XXIII

....

A retiree is on the phone getting
a new quote for his annual car insurance.
'How many miles to do you drive in a year, sir?'
asks the sales assistant.
'Oh, er, I've no idea!' replies the old chap.
'Well, is it about twenty thousand?
Ten thousand? Five thousand?'
'Oh, they all sound a lot,' the old man says.
'What month is this?'
'November, sir.'
'Ah, well maybe this will help,' he says.
'I last put petrol in it in February.'

....

One man in his time plays many parts.

William Shakespeare

Please don't retouch my wrinkles. It took me so long to earn them.

ANNA MAGNANI

....

An old couple, who are always bickering, are
having another heated discussion whilst driving on the
motorway. It's making the man drive erratically and he's
soon spotted by a patrol car. A police officer
pulls their vehicle over and walks up the driver's window.
'Can I see your licence and
registration, sir?' she asks the man.
'Ugh, what did she say?' the old man asks his wife.
'She needs to see your licence and registration, dear.'
He gets the documents out the glove box
and hands them over.
'Oh, I see you are from Brighton, sir,' she says.
'I used to have a boyfriend from
Brighton. He was the worst lover I ever had.'
'Ugh, what did she say?' the man asks his wife again.
'Nothing dear – she just thinks she used to know you.'

....

Perhaps one has to be very old before one learns to be amused rather than shocked.

Pearl S. Buck

. . . .

An 89-year-old man has some exciting
news to share with his doctor. 'I'm getting
married again next week, doc!' he says.
'Wow, that's wonderful!
And how old is the lucky lady?'
'Nineteen.'
'Well, I should warn you, too much
action under the sheets can be deadly!'
'Don't worry,' the old man says.
'If she dies, I'll just marry someone else.'

. . . .

Old age is an excellent time for outrage. My goal is to say or do at least one outrageous thing every week.

Maggie Kuhn

Well, I suppose I must attribute it to the fact that I haven't died yet.

Malcolm Sargent on being asked to what he attributed his advanced age of 70

....

An old lady answers a knock at the door.
It's the police with her husband.
'Hello madam, we found your husband in the park.
He was disorientated and asked for help to
get home, so we've given him a lift.'
She thanks the officers and closes the door.
'How did you get lost Cyril?
You've walked in that park for fifty years.'
'Not lost, exactly,' he says, sheepishly.
'Just tired of walking.'

....

Not a shred of evidence exists in favour of the idea that life is serious.

Brendan Gill

My grandmother is over 80 and still doesn't need glasses. Drinks right out of the bottle.

Henny Youngman

....

Youth is the time for adventures of the body, but age for the triumphs of the mind.

Logan Pearsall Smith

....

You'll lose your mind when you grow older. What they don't tell you is that you won't miss it very much.

Malcolm Cowley

A young man, shortly to be married, decides to
ask his grandfather's advice about sex.
'How often should I have it?' he asks.
'Oh, when you first get married you'll want it all
the time, and you might have sex several times a day.'
He then goes on to tell his grandson that after a while sex
tapers off and you have it once a week or so. Then,
as you get older, you have sex maybe once a month, and
eventually it reduces to once a year if you're lucky!
'Oh,' says the young man, taking it all in.
'So what about you and grandma now?'
'Oh, we just have oral sex now,' he says.
'Oral sex? What's that?'
'Well,' the old man says, 'She goes into her bedroom,
and I go to into my room. She yells, "F*** you!",
and I shout back, "F*** you too!"'

I think that's what makes life interesting – the evolution of getting older.

Alexis Bledel

....

The older you get, the better you get – unless you're a banana.

Ross Noble

....

I'm kind of comfortable with getting older because it's better than the other option... so I'll take getting older.

George Clooney

Fascinating fact

It seems that there's some truth
in the old adage 'age is just a number'.
A survey conducted in 2011 showed
that citizens of Greece believe that old
age arrives when you turn 68, which
presumably means that you can class
yourself as a 'youngster' right up until then!

The older we get, the better we used to be.

JOHN McENROE

Long after wearing bifocals and hearing aids, we'll still be making love. We just won't know with whom.

Jack Paar

....

A wife returns from a shopping trip to find
her retired husband waving a rolled-up
newspaper around. 'What are you doing?' she asks.
'I'm swatting flies,' he says. 'I've got
six males and two females so far.'
'How did you know what sex they were?' she says.
'Easy. Six were on my beer and
two were on the phone.

....

Sex in the sixties is great, but improves if you pull over to the side of the road.

Johnny Carson

I truly believe that age –
if you're healthy – is just a number.

Hugh Hefner

....

To be 70 years old is like climbing
the Alps. You reach a snow-crowned
summit, and see behind you the
deep valley stretching miles...

Henry Wadsworth Longfellow

....

Age is never so old as youth
would measure it.

Jack London

When grace is joined with wrinkles, it is adorable. There is an unspeakable dawn in happy old age.

Victor Hugo

....

A retired lady visits a portrait artist. 'Paint me with platinum earrings, a large diamond necklace, ruby bracelets and a sapphire broach,' she says.
'But you're not wearing any of that,'
replies the artist.
'I know,' she says. 'But if I die before my husband I'm convinced he'll remarry and I want his new bride to go nuts looking for the jewellery.'

....

As for me, except for an occasional heart attack, I feel as young as I ever did.

Robert Benchley

Two old women, Ellie and Shani, are smoking cigarettes outside their nursing home when the heavens open. Undeterred, Ellie gets a condom out of her pocket, cuts off the end, puts it over her cigarette and carries on smoking.

'What's that?' asks Shani.

'It's a condom. This way my cigarette doesn't get wet.'

'Oh, good idea, I might try that,' says Shani.

'Where did you get it?'

'You can get them at any supermarket or chemist,' says Ellie.

So the day after, Shani shuffles into the local chemist and asks the pharmacist for a packet of condoms. The pharmacist looks at her a bit oddly – she's 90 if she's a day – but politely asks what brand she would prefer.

Shani thinks for a moment. 'Oh, it doesn't matter – as long as it fits a Camel.'

A survey conducted in 2008 in the US showed that people grow happier as they grow older – up until the age of 50, life is more likely to feel troublesome, after which we start forgetting our worries and enjoying ourselves!

Laughter doesn't require teeth.

BILL NEWTON

Two medical students are in town one day when they see an old man. He appears very stiff-legged and he's walking slowly with his legs spread wide apart. The first student says to his friend, 'I'm sure that old man has Pelact Syndrome. The sufferers all walk like that.'

'No,' says the other. 'He's got Zowack Syndrome. His gait matches that condition, like we learned in class.'

They can't agree so they decide to ask the man in order to settle the argument.

'We're medical students and we couldn't help but notice the way you walk,' the first student says. 'We can't agree on which syndrome you have. I think you've got Pelact Syndrome and my friend thinks it's Zowack. Which is it?'

'You're both wrong,' replies the old man.

'What do you have then?' they ask.

'Well, I thought it was wind, but it looks like I was wrong too!'

Research in 2009 showed that the average 50-year-old is in better shape than a person half their age. At 50, a typical person will have a lower daily calorie intake and participate in a broader range of physical activities than an average 25-year-old.

KICKING BACK

It is necessary to relax your muscles when you can. Relaxing your brain is fatal.

Stirling Moss

When men reach their sixties and retire, they go to pieces. Women go right on cooking.

Gail Sheehy

....

A teen takes a shortcut home through a cemetery.
Suddenly, he's startled by a tapping noise coming
from the shadows. At first he's petrified,
but he then sees an old man with a hammer
and chisel chipping away at a headstone.
'What a relief,' says the teen, 'I thought you
were a ghost. Why are you working so late?'
'Oh, those morons,' moans the old man.
'They spelt my name wrong!'

....

Ten men waiting for me at the door? Send one of them home, I'm tired.

Mae West

A retired man is given a set of golf clubs by his co-workers
as a leaving present. He's never played before but,
with some free clubs and plenty of time now on
his hands, he thinks he'll give it a go.
He contacts the professional at his local club for lessons,
explaining that he's never touched a golf club and he's
starting from scratch. The pro shows him the basic stance,
grip and swing, then says, 'Just try to hit the ball towards
that flag in the distance.' With that, the man unleashes an
arrow-straight shot, which soars about
200 yards and comes to rest inches from the hole.
The pro is speechless.
'So, now what?' the man asks, nonchalantly.
The pro takes a couple of moments to gather himself.
'Uh...' he begins, unsteadily, 'you're supposed
to hit the ball into the hole.'
'Oh, great!' the man replies. 'Now you tell me!'

I always wake up at the crack of ice.

JOE E. LEWIS

Old men should have more care to end life well than to live long.

Anita Brookner

....

A grandma is shuffling along a beach in Spain
when she is approached by a beggar holding
out his hands in desperation. '*Por favor, Señora,*'
the poor man pleads, 'can you spare any money?
I haven't eaten all day.'
'That's good,' says the grandma.
'Now you won't have to worry about
cramps when you go swimming.'

....

It is true you are gently shouldered off the stage, but then you are given such a comfortable front stall as spectator.

Confucius on old age

Feeling edgy and a bit unwell, an old man
takes a hot bath. He just gets himself settled when the
doorbell rings. He dries himself off, puts on a dressing
gown and some slippers and heads downstairs to answer
the door. It's someone trying to sell life insurance.
Exasperated, he slams the door and returns to the bath.
Three minutes later the doorbell goes again.
'Oh, hell,' he shouts, infuriated. Back on with the
dressing gown. Back on with the slippers. But as he steps
forward he slips on a wet spot, falls and hits his back on
the side of the bath. Swearing under his breath,
he drives to the doctor in agony.
'You're lucky – it could be a lot worse,' says the doctor,
after examining the man's back.
'Nothing is broken, but I think you need to relax.
Why don't you go home and take a long, hot bath?'

Live each day as if it were your last, and garden as though you will live forever.

Anonymous

....

A pensioner, lazy and penny-pinching, finally buys a ride-on lawnmower to tackle his huge garden. 'This thing is brilliant,' he says to his neighbour one day. 'It's only taken me an hour to mow the whole lawn. It used to take my wife the best part of the week!'

....

The golden age is before us, not behind us.

William Shakespeare

If you associate enough with older people who enjoy their lives, you will gain the possibility for a full life.

Margaret Mead

. . . .

Retirement at 65 is ridiculous. When I was 65 I still had pimples.

George Burns

. . . .

Life has got to be lived. That's all there is to it.

Eleanor Roosevelt

Fascinating fact

The chilled-out art of t'ai chi has been
shown to improve the health of older
people. The gentle form of exercise
improves breathing, relaxation and
overall well-being – so there's really
no need to bust a gut to stay fit!

*Every wrinkle but
a notch in the
quiet calendar of a
well-spent life.*

CHARLES DICKENS

Seventy-five-year-old George visits the
doctor for his annual check-up.
'So, how have you been feeling?' asks the doctor.
'Fine,' George replies. 'I have to get up to use the toilet
more times in the night than I used to, but otherwise
OK. Mind you,' he continues. 'I think God knows that my
eyesight isn't what it was – these days he turns on the
light when I pee, and turns it off again when I've finished!'
The following day the doctor phones George to give him his
results. He's not in, so he speaks to his wife, Sally, instead.
'Your husband's test results were fine, but he did say
something strange yesterday that has been bugging me. He
claims that God turns the light on and off for him
when he uses the bathroom at night.
Do you know anything about that?'
'Yes,' says Sally, with a weary sigh.
'The silly old git's been peeing in the fridge again!'

You can't turn back the clock. But you can wind it up again.

Bonnie Prudden

....

A grandad visiting his family one afternoon asks his grandson for the household Wi-Fi password so he can check the local post office opening hours. 'Oh, it's taped under the router,' the kid tells him. Twenty minutes and various failed attempts later, he asks, 'Hang on. Am I spelling this right? T-A-P-E-D-U-N-D-E-R-T-H-E-R-O-U-T-E-R?'

....

For us elderly people, not owning a computer is like not having a headache.

Edward Enfield

My crown is called content,
a crown that seldom kings enjoy.

William Shakespeare

·····································

If you enjoy living, it is not difficult
to keep the sense of wonder.

Ray Bradbury

·····································

A man has reached middle age when
he is warned to slow down by his
doctor rather than the police.

Henny Youngman

When a man retires, his wife gets twice the husband but only half the income.

Chi-Chi Rodríguez

....

Two old-timers Ron and Amir are sitting in the pub. They fancy another drink, but neither can remember whose round it is. The discussion quickly gets heated, and pretty soon the other regulars have to intervene to stop them coming to blows. 'That's it,' says Ron eventually, as he storms out. 'I'm so mad I'm taking you off my pallbearer list.'

....

People are always asking about the good old days. I say, why don't you say the good now days?

Robert M. Young

Two strangers are sitting together on a plane.
'Hi! I'm Julie,' says one. 'I'm flying to Scotland for my
granddaughter's fourth birthday. It's so exciting –
I remember when she was only this big and now she's four.
I can't believe it. She's adorable. Hang on, I've got a picture
of her. Look. Oh, couldn't you just cuddle her forever?
And she's doing so well at nursery. She's the best in her
class, she can count to twenty now and even knows
some of the alphabet. Oh, it gets me all teary eyed...'
After about half an hour of this, Julie realises she's been
rather impolite, rambling on and on to the poor man sat
next to her. 'Oh, I'm sorry,' she says. 'Listen to me.
I haven't let you get a word in edgeways!
Tell me... what do you think about my granddaughter?'

Housework can't kill you, but why take a chance?

PHYLLIS DILLER

It is true that whisky improves with age. The older I get, the more I like it.

Ronnie Corbett

....

A local musician entertains patients in nursing homes and hospitals. At one such hospital he tells some jokes, plays his keyboard and sings some silly songs at the patients' bedsides. When he's finished he bids farewell and says, 'I hope you all get better soon.' One old gentleman shoots back, 'And I hope you get better, too.'

....

A man is not old as long as he is seeking something.

Jean Rostand

A frail, elderly lady arrives at a nursing home one evening.
Her family kisses her goodbye and say they'll visit her the
next day. The following morning, the nurses get her out of
bed, bathe her, feed her breakfast and sit her in front of a
bay window with a beautiful view of the flower garden.
All seems well, but after a few minutes she
slowly starts leaning over sideways in her chair.
A couple of nurses rush to her aid, catching
her and straightening her up on some pillows.
The next few minutes are fine but then the old lady starts
tilting the other way. Again the nurses spring into action
and straighten her up. This continues for several hours.
Later in the afternoon the woman's son pops by to see her.
'So, Mum, have you settled in OK?
Are they treating you well?' he asks.
'It's pretty good,' she replies.
'Except they won't let you fart.'

Do not worry about
avoiding temptation.
As you grow older
it will avoid you.

JOEY ADAMS

I think all old folks' homes should have striptease. If I ran one I'd have a striptease every week.

Cynthia Payne

....

A grandad is reminiscing to his grandson.
'When I was young,' he says, 'my mother could
send me shopping with fifty pence,
and I would return with three loaves of bread,
two pints of milk, a dozen eggs and a few
slices of ham. Can't do it these days...'
'Why's that?' asks the grandson.
'Too many security cameras.'

....

Every morning, like clockwork, at 7 a.m., I pee. Unfortunately, I don't wake up till 8.

Anonymous

Most would agree that a little doze does a lot of good. In support of this, statistics have shown that men and women who nap at least three times a week have a 37 per cent lower coronary mortality rate than those who don't.

The first sign of maturity is the discovery that the volume knob also turns to the left.

JERRY M. WRIGHT

A massage is just like a movie... except in a massage you're the star. And you don't miss anything by falling asleep!

Elizabeth Jane Howard

....

How beautiful it is to do nothing and then to rest afterward.

Spanish proverb

....

Since people are going to be living longer and getting older, they'll just have to learn how to be babies longer.

Andy Warhol

Edie goes to the undertakers to visit the body of
her late husband. When the mortician pulls back the sheet
she starts sobbing – Abdul is wearing a black suit but
it was his dying wish to be buried in a blue suit.
The mortician says he's sorry, that bodies are traditionally
dressed in black, and that he will try to rectify it.
The next day she returns to have one last moment with Abdul
prior to the funeral. This time when the mortician pulls back
the sheet, she smiles. He looks perfect in a blue suit.
'Oh, that's wonderful, thank you. Where did you get the suit?'
'Well, fortunately, a man about your husband's size came in
wearing a blue suit,' the mortician replies. 'His wife was upset
because she wanted him buried in the traditional black suit.'
Edie smiles at the undertaker. He continues,
'After that, it was really just a matter of swapping the heads.'

Middle age is having a choice between two temptations and choosing the one that'll get you home earlier.

Dan Bennett

....

Two elderly sisters are looking at the invitation to a ballroom night at their village hall. 'It says here we've got to wear an outfit that matches our husband's hair, so I'm wearing black,' says one. 'Oh, crikey,' says the other. 'I'd better not go.'

....

I always make a point of starting the day at 6 a.m. with champagne. It goes straight to the heart and cheers one up.

John Mortimer

My idea of a good night out is a good night in.

JACK ROSENTHAL

Do I exercise? Well I once
jogged to the ashtray.

Will Self

....

A little nonsense now and then,
is relished by the wisest men.

Roald Dahl

....

The good thing about getting older
is that... you have less desire to go
out and conquer everyone you see.

Julian Clary

Harry, long since retired from the office, decides to try his hand at farming very late in life. He buys a herd of cows and then introduces a bull to do some breeding. But all does not go according to plan. After a few days he moans to his friend, 'That bull is only interested in eating grass. It won't even look at a cow.'
'Why don't you take him to the vet then?' his friend suggests.
A few days later and Harry is much happier. 'The vet gave me some pills,' he tells his pal. 'I gave them to the bull yesterday, and not only has the randy bugger serviced all of my cows, but he broke down the fence and mated with my neighbour's herd too! He's rampant.'
'Wow, what kind of pills were they?' asks his friend.
'I don't know, but they tasted of peppermint.'

Fascinating fact

It seems that laughter really is the best medicine. The simple act of laughing has been shown to have considerable health benefits for young and old, as the physical actions involved help to decrease stress, increase pain tolerance and, of course, reduce depression!

*I don't want to retire.
I'm not that good
at crossword puzzles.*

NORMAN MAILER

Cherish all your happy moments;
they make a fine cushion for old age.

Booth Tarkington

....

Older people shouldn't eat health foods.
They need all the preservatives
they can get.

Robert Orben

....

Sometimes I sits and thinks,
and sometimes I just sits.

Satchel Paige

You're never too old to rock 'n' roll!
It's estimated that one in five festival goers
in Britain are over 50, helped perhaps
by the amount of over-fifties festivals
held around the country.

BIRTHDAY BLUES

For all the advances in medicine, there is still no cure for the common birthday.

John Glenn

A group of 40-year-old friends discuss where they should meet for dinner. Finally, they decide on Restaurant Gaston because the waitresses there are always pretty and wear low-cut tops. Ten years later, aged 50, they discuss locations for the next reunion and again agree to eat at Restaurant Gaston because they know the food and wine there is very good. Ten years later, aged 60, they decide to meet again at Restaurant Gaston because it's peaceful and smoke free. Another decade later, and aged 70, the group has another reunion and they discuss where to meet. They decide on Restaurant Gaston because it has good wheelchair access and a lift. Finally, ten years later, when they're 80, they meet up again. This time they decide to eat at Restaurant Gaston because none of them have ever been there before and it'll make a nice change.

A diplomat is a man
who always remembers
a woman's birthday
but never remembers
her age.

ROBERT FROST

Oh, to be 70 again.

Georges Clemenceau on seeing a pretty girl on his eightieth birthday

....

For a grandmother's ninety-fifth birthday,
her family arrange to have a photo announcement
printed in the local paper. The lady's son
is reviewing the paper at her party.
'That's a nice picture, Mum' he says.
'Yes. It's my passport picture,' she replies.
'Really?' The son didn't realise she'd been
abroad recently. 'Where did you go?'
'The post office.'

....

There is no cure for birth and death, save to enjoy the interval.

George Santayana

I want to live to be 80 so
I can piss more people off.

Charles Bukowski

....

The years that a woman subtracts
from her age are not lost. They are
added to the ages of other women.

Diane de Poitiers

....

Eventually you will reach a point
when you stop lying about your age
and start bragging about it.

Will Rogers

My wife hasn't had a birthday in four years. She was born in the year of Lord-only-knows.

Anonymous

. . . .

During celebrations for his one hundred and first birthday party, the old man is asked by a guest if he thinks he'll be around for his one hundred and second.
'Oh, I sure do,' he replies. 'Statistics show that hardly anyone dies between the ages of a hundred and one and a hundred and two.'

. . . .

Middle age is when you've met so many people that every new person you meet reminds you of someone else.

Ogden Nash

For her one hundred and second birthday, Bess Tancrelle, along with her 97-year-old sister in the sidecar, realised her dream of riding a Harley-Davidson motorcycle. On the back of her helmet she placed a sticker with the message, 'Screw it, let's ride.'

Three grannies are sitting on a bench near their nursing home.
An old man walks past them. 'Hey,' shouts one of the old women.
'We bet you we can guess exactly how old you are.'
The man is a bit annoyed by the heckling,
'There's no way you can tell.'
Another of the grannies says, 'Yes we can!
Just drop your trousers and pants and we'll
be able to tell. Bet you five pounds.'
The man is rather embarrassed, but he's determined to prove
them wrong and make some money so he goes ahead.
The grannies get him to twirl round and jump up and
down a few times. After a couple of minutes of this they
yell in unison, 'You're eighty-three years old!'
The man is gobsmacked. Standing there, still with his pants
around his ankles, he asks, 'How on earth did you guess?'
Laughing, they shout: 'We were at your
birthday party yesterday, Harold!'

There are 364 days
when you might get
un-birthday presents...
and only one for
birthday presents,
you know.

LEWIS CARROLL

We know we're getting old when the only thing we want for our birthday is not to be reminded of it.

Anonymous

....

An elderly couple, both 93, arrive a local
restaurant for lunch and wait to be seated.
The maître d' greets them:
'Do you have a reservation?'
'No we don't,' says the old man.
'Ah, in that case,' says the maître d'
'it could be at least a fifty minute wait.'
'Young man, we're both ninety-three years old,'
he tells the maître d'.
'We might not have fifty minutes.'

....

Birthdays are nature's way of telling us to eat more cake.

Anonymous

No woman should ever be quite accurate about her age. It looks so calculating.

Oscar Wilde

. . . .

Last week the candle factory burned down. Everyone just stood around and sang 'Happy Birthday'.

Steven Wright

. . . .

Old age is always 15 years older than I am.

Oliver Wendell Holmes Sr

A rich old lady from London is preparing her will. She tells her lawyer she has two requests. Firstly, she has to be cremated, and secondly, she needs her ashes scattered in Harrods. 'Harrods!' says the lawyer in surprise. 'Why on earth there?' 'Because then my daughters are bound to visit me every week.'

I'm not interested in age.
People who tell me their age are silly.
You're as old as you feel.

Elizabeth Arden

. . . .

Two dear friends spot each other
on the high street. After exchanging
pleasantries for a couple of minutes, one says,
'Listen, this is really embarrassing, but I've
forgotten your name. What is it?'
The other stares back at him
and eventually says, 'Um, I'm going to
have to get back to you on that.'

. . . .

Every year on your birthday,
you get a chance to start new.

Sammy Hagar

A 95-year-old Englishman arrives at the airport in Paris. Being rather frail and slow, he takes a while to locate his passport at Customs, much to the chagrin of the customs officer.

'You have been to France before, monsieur?' the customs officer asks, with a sarcastic tone.

The old man tells him that, yes, he has been once before.

'Then surely you should know that you need to get your passport ready for inspection.'

'No, actually,' the old man replies. 'Last time I was here I didn't have to show it.'

'That cannot be true, monsieur – everyone has to show their passport when they enter France.'

The old man gives him a cold, hard stare and explains: 'Well, my apologies, but when I came ashore at Juno Beach on D-Day in 1944 to help liberate this country, I couldn't find any Frenchmen to show it to.'

Never worry about your
heart till it stops beating.

E. B. White

....

You can't stop the ageing process.
There's only so much oil
you can put on your body.

Angie Dickinson

....

Age is just a number.
It's totally irrelevant unless, of course,
you happen to be a bottle of wine.

Joan Collins

*I just tell people
I'm as old as my wife.
Then I lie about her age.*

FRED METCALF

Let us celebrate the occasion with wine and sweet words.

Plautus on birthdays

....

An elderly shopper goes into a chemist to stock up
on make-up. When she gets to the till her basket is
brimming over with goods and she needs
help lifting it. The shop assistant notices her
written list and sees that cold cream,
cotton balls, cotton swabs, lipstick, concealer
and powder are all under the heading, 'Repairs.'

....

A woman has the right to treat the subject of her age with ambiguity.

Helena Rubinstein

Eager to make it a day to remember, a husband asks his wife what she'd like for her forthcoming sixtieth birthday. 'Oh, I'd love to be ten again,' she says. The husband ponders her request for a few days and comes up with a plan. Come the day, he wakes her up with a breakfast in bed of chocolate pancakes, takes her to the local amusement park to go on all the rides and finishes in the evening with a children's film and a big ice cream with a flake. 'So, how was it today?' the husband asks when they are lying in bed that night. 'It was pretty good,' his wife says. 'Certainly a surprise. But when I said I wanted to be ten again, I meant my dress size.'

I believe in loyalty.
When a woman reaches an age
she likes she should stick to it.

Eva Gabor

. . . .

A seventy-something man goes to the
doctors in late December one year. During idle
conversation the physician asks him with a smile,
'So, was Santa good to you this year?'
'Oh, yes, really good,' says the old man.
'I got an SUV.'
'Wow, nice.'
'Yeah... Socks, Underwear and Viagra.'

. . . .

It is so comic to hear oneself
called old, even at 90 I suppose!

Alice James

Fascinating fact

Apparently determined to party away the birthday blues, the Sultan of Brunei's fiftieth birthday party cost a whopping $27.2 million (£17.4 million) and included three concerts – one featuring Michael Jackson. That's enough to make the average birthday celebration seem like the bargain of the year!

The key to successful ageing is to pay
as little attention to it as possible.

Judith Regan

. . . .

The best birthdays are all those
that haven't arrived yet.

Robert Orben

. . . .

There is only one cure for grey hair.
It was invented by a Frenchman.
It is called the guillotine.

P. G. Wodehouse

I found my first grey hair today. On my chest.

Wendy Liebman

. . . .

It's the eve of Betty's sixtieth birthday.
Her husband, Dave, is two years older.
Keen to dish out some gentle ribbing about her age
milestone he sits her down, looks deep into
her eyes, and says, 'I've never made love to
anyone who was over sixty years old.'
'Oh, well, I have,' she says flatly.
'And it's really not that great.'

. . . .

Age ain't nothing but a number, so I feel good.

Denzel Washington

Why is a birthday cake the only food you can blow on... and everybody rushes to get a piece?

BOBBY KELTON

The older I get, the older old is.

Tom Baker

....

A grandad is bending over to tie the shoelaces
of his four-year-old granddaughter. Little Alice
starts staring at the top of his head, then touches a
badly thinning area of hair. She seems concerned.
'I think you've got a hole in your head, grandad,' she
says. 'Does it hurt you?'
Grandad pauses, then replies, 'No, not physically.'

....

Age seldom arrives smoothly or quickly. It's more often a succession of jerks.

Jean Rhys

A very frail man is lying on his deathbed upstairs. While he lies there, gasping for each breath, he is sure he can smell freshly-baked chocolate chip cookies – his most favourite food in all the world. 'I must be dreaming it,' he thinks. But it seems so real. So, with every ounce of strength that he can muster, he crawls out of bed and very slowly hobbles down the stairs. The delicious smell gets stronger with each step. Sure enough, as he turns the corner he sees a huge plate of chocolate chip cookies on the table at the far side of the kitchen. He continues shuffling towards them, even though he is in terrible pain. When he finally makes it to the table and reaches towards one of the cookies with a trembling hand, his wife rushes in, slaps his hand and shouts, 'DON'T TOUCH THOSE – they're for the funeral!'

As the talk turns to old age,
I say I am 49 plus VAT.

Lionel Blair

....

When you're 50, you start thinking
about things you haven't thought about
before... Getting wrinkles is trivial.

Eugene O'Neill

....

At 65... there are only two things
you can do: laugh or kill yourself.

John Le Carré

Fascinating fact

Floyd Creekmore, working under the name Creeky, was recognised as the oldest working clown in February 2012 at 95 years of age. An added bonus of being a clown, of course, is that he wouldn't have to pay out for any entertainment on his birthday!

Birthdays are good for you. Statistics show that the people who have the most live the longest.

ANONYMOUS

**Our birthdays are feathers
in the broad wing of time.**

Jean Paul Richter

....

**There is more felicity on the far side
of baldness than young men
can possibly imagine.**

Logan Pearsall Smith

....

**As a young man, I used to have four
supple members and a stiff one.
Now I have four stiff and one supple.**

Henri Duc D'Aumale

By the time they reach 60, three in five men and two in five women will be snorers. So think twice the next time you get the urge to wedge a sock in your partner's mouth when they're shaking the windows with their snoring!

GETTING PHYSICAL

Life expectancy would grow by leaps and bounds if green vegetables smelled as good as bacon.

Doug Larson

An elderly couple go to see the doctor. 'We want to know if we are making love properly,' says the man. 'Will you look at us doing it and let us know?' The doctor reluctantly agrees. The couple get undressed, lie down on the bed and make love. 'Well?' says the man, afterwards. 'You are making love perfectly,' the doctor says. 'That will be ten pounds.' They return every week for six weeks and go through the whole thing again each time. 'I don't understand this,' says the doctor on their seventh visit. 'I told you that you were making love properly the first time, yet you keep coming back.' 'She can't come to my house,' says the man, 'and I can't go to hers. A hotel costs twenty pounds. You charge us a tenner and we get eight quid back on insurance.'

After 30, a body has a mind of its own.

Bette Midler

....

Two old guys are chewing the fat one day.
One turns to the other and says: 'You know,
Bill, I'm almost ninety now and
really feeling my age. How are you doing?'
'I feel just like a newborn baby actually,' Bill replies.
'Really? How so?'
'Well, I'm bald, I've got no teeth and
I'm fairly sure I just peed myself.'

....

I'm in pretty good shape
for the shape I'm in.

Mickey Rooney

*I really don't think
I need buns of steel.
I'd be happy with
buns of cinnamon.*

ELLEN DeGENERES

Advanced old age is when you sit in a rocking chair and can't get it going.

Golda Meir

....

An elderly couple visit the doctor to discuss
their sex life. 'So what's the problem?'
the doctor asks the husband.
'Well, the first time I make love to my wife,
all is fine. But, the second time, I get very sweaty.'
'Hmm. Can you think of any reason
for this?' he asks the wife.
'Yes. The first time is in February
and the second is in August.'

....

A man's health can be judged by which he takes two at a time – pills or stairs.

Joan Welsh

A senior citizen goes to the doctor. 'Doc, I'm in
severe pain all over. Everywhere I touch hurts.'
'I see,' says the doctor. 'Let's test this
out, then. Touch your knee.'
The man touches his knee and screams in agony. The doctor's
surprised. 'OK then, now touch the top of your head.'
The guy touches his head and jumps and yelps in pain. Next the
doctor asks him to touch his elbow. Once again the man is in
huge discomfort. Wherever he touches, it hurts like hell.
The doctor is confused and orders a complete set of X-rays.
Two days later the man comes back in for the
results, still no better than he was before.
'Well, we've found the problem,' announces the doctor.
'Oh, great. What is it?' asks the old man.
'You've broken your finger!'

The trouble with always
trying to preserve the
health of the body is
that it is so difficult to
do without destroying
the health of the mind.

G. K. CHESTERTON

The need of exercise is a modern superstition, invented by people who ate too much and had nothing to think about.

George Santayana

....

I wish I had the energy that my grandchildren have – if only for self-defence.

Gene Perret

....

I still have a full deck; I just shuffle slower now.

Anonymous

At 81, Ernestine Shepherd is the world's oldest (competitive female) bodybuilder and holds a Guinness World Record to prove it. She gets up at 3.00 a.m. to start her day of training, which involves working out, lifting weights and a 10-mile run!

A young man is out jogging when he spots an old chap sitting
on a park bench, crying his eyes out. He stops to ask him what's
wrong. 'Oh, I can't bear it,' he begins. 'I've got a twenty-one-
year-old wife at home. She massages my back in the bath
every morning, then makes me a slap-up breakfast.
Then she cleans the house while I sit around watching TV.'
'So why are you crying?' the young man asks.
'She makes me homemade soup for lunch
and my favourite brownies, then carries my
golf clubs round the course every afternoon.'
'Well, why are you crying?' the young chap persists.
'For dinner she makes me a four course gourmet meal with wine
and then makes love with me every night until the early hours.'
'So, why on earth are you crying?'
says the young man, bemused.
'I can't remember where I live!'

*Between two evils,
I always pick the one
I never tried before.*

MAE WEST

Fitness – if it came in a bottle, everybody would have a great body.

Cher

. . . .

A grandma has just finished eating her
Sunday lunch. She gets up and goes to the sink,
watched by her young grandson. He's flabbergasted
when she reaches into her mouth, carefully
takes out her dentures, brushes and rinses them,
and then pops them back in.
'Wow, that's awesome, Grandma!' he says.
'Now take off your leg!'

. . . .

My idea of exercise is a good brisk sit.

Phyllis Diller

There's a lot of people in
this world who spend so much time
watching their health that they
haven't the time to enjoy it.

Josh Billings

. . . .

As you get older, the pickings get
slimmer, but the people don't.

Carrie Fisher

. . . .

Time is a dressmaker
specialising in alterations.

Faith Baldwin

My doctor told me to do something that puts me out of breath, so I've taken up smoking again.

Jo Brand

....

An old man goes into a chemist.
'Two Viagra pills,' he says, 'but can
you please cut them in half?'
'Sure, but you do realise they won't
be as effective in a fifty per cent dosage?'
'Oh, yes,' the old man replies. 'But I don't
need them for sex. I just want to get myself
hard enough so I don't piss on my shoes.'

....

You know you've reached middle age when your weightlifting consists merely of standing up.

Bob Hope

*No cowboy was ever
faster on the draw
than a grandparent
pulling a baby picture
out of a wallet.*

ANONYMOUS

On the morning of their anniversary an old couple
are sitting at the table, eating breakfast and thinking back over
their 50 years of marriage. 'Just think, love,' says the husband,
'we've been married for fifty years today.'
'Yes,' she replies, 'Fifty years ago we were
sitting here at this breakfast table together.'
'I know,' he says, 'But we were wild and carefree back then.
We probably would have sat here eating in the nude.'
'Well, what d'ya say?' the wife giggles. 'Shall we strip
down again for old time's sake?' So the pair strip to
the buff and sit back down at the table.
'You know, honey,' the little old lady says breathlessly
after a few moments, 'My nipples are as hot for
you today as they were fifty years ago.'
'I'm not surprised,' replies her husband.
'One's in your coffee and the other's in your porridge!'

The first time I see a jogger smiling, I'll consider it.

Joan Rivers

....

Three elderly women are sitting on a park bench having a natter when, bold as brass, a flasher approaches them and opens his coat as wide as it will go. The first old lady had a stroke, followed quickly by the second.
The third little old lady couldn't reach.

....

Men chase golf balls when they're too old to chase anything else.

Groucho Marx

To win back my youth... there is nothing I wouldn't do – except take exercise, get up early, or be a useful member of the community.

Oscar Wilde

....

An old couple, both in their eighties, are getting ready to go to sleep. The old man lies on the bed as usual when he notices his wife lying on the floor. 'What are you doing down there, dear? he asks. 'I just want to feel something hard for a change,' she says.

....

They say that age is all in your mind. The trick is keeping it from creeping down into your body.

Anonymous

Swimming and cycling are two activities recommended for those who are getting on a bit. The advantage of both of these forms of exercise is that they don't put undue pressure on the joints. If you're not so good at swimming, there's always the shallow end – and no one ever forgets how to ride a bike!

I have the body of an 18-year-old.
I keep it in the fridge.

SPIKE MILLIGAN

· ·

An old lady is leafing through a magazine
looking for inspiration for a new hairstyle.
She sees something she likes on a beautiful
young model. Wanting a second opinion,
she shows the page to her husband.
'Do you think this style would
suit a face with a few wrinkles?' she asks.
He looks at the picture, crumples it up,
straightens it out and studies it again.
'Yes. Should be fine, darling.'

· ·

I knew I was going bald when
it was taking me longer and
longer to wash my face.

Harry Hill

. . . .

As you get older three things happen.
The first is your memory goes,
and I can't remember the other two.

Norman Wisdom

. . . .

I am pushing 60.
That is enough exercise for me.

Mark Twain

An elderly lady goes to the doctor to discuss her sex life.
'I haven't had sex for years,' she says. 'Is there anything
I can do to increase my husband's sex drive?'
'Have you tried Viagra?' says the doctor, helpfully.
She frowns. 'He hates medication.
I can't even get him to take headache pills.'
'OK,' says the doctor, 'why don't you crush the Viagra into
a powder? Slip it into his drink and he'll be none the wiser.'
'Good idea,' she says.
Three days later the lady returns and she's not happy.
'So how did it go?' asks the doctor, nervously.
'Oh, dreadfully.'
'Why? Didn't it work?'
'Oh, yes,' the old lady says. 'It worked. I did as you told me. He got
straight up, ripped off his clothes and then mine and we made love
right there on the table. It was the best sex I've ever had.'
'What's the problem, then?' asks the doctor.
'Well,' she says, 'I'll never be able to show
my face in our local pub again.'

I'm at an age when my back
goes out more than I do.

Phyllis Diller

....

Better to hunt in fields,
for health unbought,
Than fee the doctor for
a nauseous draught.

John Dryden

....

Exercise daily. Eat wisely.
Die anyway.

Anonymous

Fascinating fact

Fauja Singh, the Turbaned Tornado, believed to be the world's oldest marathon runner, ran his first marathon (London) at the age of 89 in 2000, and at the age of 101, ran what he has said will be his last marathon (also London) in 2012. He was an honorary starter at the Birmingham International Marathon in 2017 at the age of 106.
He holds many records but Guinness World Records cannot certify his records because Fauja cannot find a birth certificate!

Fibroids — isn't that a breakfast cereal?

VICTORIA WOOD

My mother is no spring chicken although she has got as many chemicals in her as one.

Barry Humphries

....

Interviewer: Can you remember
any of your past lives?
The Dalai Lama: At my age I have a problem
remembering what happened yesterday.

....

And in the end it's not the years in your life that count. It's the life in your years.

Edward J. Stieglitz

Whenever I feel like exercise, I lie down until the feeling passes.

Robert M. Hutchins

....

Gladys and her fellow pensioner
Deirdre meet for a cup of coffee.
'Oh, you've got a new locket,' says Deirdre,
sipping her drink. 'That's pretty. Have you
got a memento in there?'
'Yes, as a matter of fact I've got a
lock of my husband's hair.'
'But Billy's not dead!'
'No, I know, but his hair is long gone.'

....

I'd like to learn to ski but I'm 44 and I'm worried about my knees. They creak a lot and I'm afraid they might start an avalanche.

Jonathan Ross

My doctor says I should... get more fresh air and exercise. I said, 'All right, I'll drive with the car window open.'

Angus Walker

....

Ray and Irene tie the knot very late in life. On the first night of their honeymoon they're getting into bed, preparing to have sex for the first time when Irene says, 'I should tell you I have acute angina.' 'Oh, I do hope so,' replies Ray, 'because your boobs aren't much to write home about.'

....

Someone asked someone who was about my age: 'How are you?' The answer was, 'Fine. If you don't ask for details.'

Katharine Hepburn

Doris Long, 101, broke her own world record for being the oldest person to abseil when she abseiled down the Spinnaker Tower in Portsmouth in 2015.

OLDER AND WISER

If age imparted wisdom,
there wouldn't be any old fools.

Claudia Young

*Old age is like
a plane flying through
a storm. Once you're
aboard, there's nothing
you can do.*

GOLDA MEIR

An old couple visit the doctor, worried that they're both losing their memories. The doctor suggests writing little notes so they don't forget things. It's about lunchtime when they get home, so the wife says, 'Darling can you go to the kitchen and make me a cheese sandwich please? Why don't you write it down so you don't forget?'

'Come on, my memory's not that bad!' the husband replies.

'I think I can remember a cheese sandwich.'

'Well, I'd also like ham, lettuce, cucumber and mayonnaise in it actually.'

'Sure,' he says. 'A cheese, ham, lettuce, cucumber and mayonnaise sandwich coming right up.'

After about half an hour of cupboard doors opening and closing and pots and pans banging, the husband finally emerges holding a bowl of ice cream.

His wife looks at him in horror. 'Oh, Brian,' she rages, 'where're the strawberries?'

The person who is too old to learn was probably always too old to learn.

Caryl Haskins

....

Pensioners Derek and Sue are devoted churchgoers. After settling into their seats for one Sunday service, Sue squirms uncomfortably. She leans towards Derek and whispers: 'I've just done a silent fart. I don't know what to do. Any suggestions?'
'Yes,' her husband replies.
'Replace the battery in your hearing aid.'

....

As I get older, I get smaller. I see other parts of the world I didn't see before.

Neil Young

The more sand has escaped from the hourglass of our life, the clearer we should see through it.

Niccolò Machiavelli

....

To keep the heart unwrinkled, to be hopeful, kindly, cheerful, reverent – that is to triumph over old age.

Thomas Bailey Aldrich

....

To know how to grow old is the master work of wisdom, and one of the most difficult chapters in the great art of living.

Henri-Frédéric Amiel

Ingeborg Rapoport is the oldest person to have ever been awarded a doctorate, aged 102. She was a 25-year-old PHD student at the University of Hamburg, but was prevented from defending her thesis at the time by the Nazis. Seventy-seven years later she got her chance and impressed the committee.

Shortly after her eighty-fifth birthday
a lady receives a notice for jury
service in the post, despite being
far too old. She phones the office
to tell them she is exempt.
'You need to fill out the exemption
form then,' the clerk says.
'But I filled it out last year.'
'You have to fill them out
every year,' he persists.
'Why? Do you think I'm getting younger?'

Experience is a terrible teacher who sends horrific bills.

Anonymous

....

In the pharmacy, the shop assistant
approaches an old lady who looks a bit lost.
'Can I help you find anything?' he says.
'Yes. How about a face cream that actually
reduces wrinkles,' jokes the old woman.
'We keep that in the back, next to world peace
and the shelf of winning lottery tickets.'

....

Old age is ready to undertake tasks that youth shirked because they would take too long.

W. Somerset Maugham

I never dared be radical
when young for fear
it would make me
conservative when old.

ROBERT FROST

An elderly lady visits the doctor to discuss
a delicate matter. 'I can't seem to stop passing
wind, doctor, but it doesn't affect me too much.
It never smells and it's always silent. As a matter
of fact, I've passed gas at least thirty times
since I've been sitting here.'
'Hmm, I see,' the doctor says. 'This is an interesting
case. Please take these pills three times a day
with meals and come back to see me next week.
Then we'll see how things are going.'
The next week the lady returns, as requested.
'Doctor,' she begins, 'I don't know what was in those
pills, but now, although my wind is still silent,
it really stinks.'
'Good, that's as I'd hoped', the doctor replies. 'Now
that we seem to have cleared out your
sinuses we can start to work on your hearing.'

Age is opportunity no less than youth itself.

Henry Wadsworth Longfellow

....

An elderly retiree hobbles gingerly into
an ice cream parlour, ooh-ing and ahh-ing all
the way. Slowly and carefully, he climbs onto a
stool, grimaces some more then orders
a strawberry sundae.
'Crushed nuts?' asks the server.
'No,' he says. 'Bad knees.'

....

You don't get older, you get better.

Shirley Bassey

The elderly don't drive that badly; they're just the only ones with time to do the speed limit.

Jason Love

....

I've reached an age when I can't use my youth as an excuse for my ignorance any more.

Janet Bonellie

....

Don't just count your years, make your years count.

Ernest Myers

I don't need you to remind me of my age, I have a bladder to do that for me.

Stephen Fry

....

A class of fifteen-year-olds are given an assignment to interview an 'old person' about his or her life. Nadiya asks her grandma a list of questions including, 'What was the biggest historical event that happened during your childhood?' 'Well, I'd have to say the moonwalk,' she replies. Nadiya looks disappointed. 'Was that dance really so important to you?'

....

We are not limited by our old age; we are liberated by it.

Stu Mittleman

*When people are old
enough to know better,
they're old enough
to do worse.*

HESKETH PEARSON

Two American men get talking in a bar. One is young and up-and-coming, the other very old and filthy rich. The young man asks the old guy how he made all his money. 'Well, son,' says the man stroking his beard, 'it was nineteen thirty-two. The midst of the Great Depression. I was down to my last nickel. I invested that nickel in an apple. I spent all day polishing the apple and, at the end of the day, I sold the apple for ten cents. The next morning, I used those ten cents to buy two more apples. Once again, I spent the whole day polishing them and sold them before nightfall for twenty cents. I stuck by this system for four weeks and by the end I'd accumulated a fortune of one dollar seventy-five.' 'Wow. And that's how you built your empire?' the young man asks. 'Hell, no!' the man replies. 'Then my wife's father passed away and left us five million dollars.'

A good head and a good heart are always a formidable combination.

Nelson Mandela

....

If nothing is going well, call your grandmother.

Italian proverb

....

There's no fool like an old fool... you can't beat experience.

Jacob M. Braude

Learning sleeps and snores in libraries, but wisdom is everywhere, wide awake, on tiptoes.

Josh Billings

....

An elderly seamstress is slowly making her way back to work after her lunch break. She's suddenly startled by a flasher who leaps out of an alley and pulls his mac wide open. The old woman studies him carefully up and down, shakes her head and says 'You call that a lining?'

....

The best part of the art of living is to know how to grow old gracefully.

Eric Hoffer

Experience is a comb that life gives you after you lose your hair.

Judith Stern

....

An elderly woman complains to her doctor about
not being able to hear out of her left ear.
The doctor shines a light in, then takes some
tweezers and pulls something out. 'It seems you
inserted a suppository into your ear,' he says.
'Ah,' the old lady replies. 'I guess that explains
why I can't find my hearing aid!'

....

They told me if I got older I'd get wiser. In that case I must be a genius.

George Burns

A retired American man goes to the Social Security office
to apply for his veteran's allowance. The lady at the counter
asks to see his driver's licence so she can check his age.
He awkwardly pats round his pockets. 'I'm very sorry, I've left
my wallet at home. Am I going to have to drive back and get it?'
'Well, usually yes,' says the woman, 'but let's try
something else. Unbutton your shirt for me.'
He does, and in so doing reveals a mass of curly grey hair.
'Ah, that grey hair is all the proof I need,' says the lady,
and processes his application without future ado.
When the man gets home, he recounts
the strange story to his wife.
'Oh!' she says, irritated. 'If you'd have dropped your trousers,
she might have given you a disability benefit too.'

Arthur Dake was a chess grandmaster
and continued to play in rated tournaments
until he passed away at the age of 89.

From birth to age 18,
a girl needs good
parents... from 55 on,
she needs cash.

SOPHIE TUCKER

He who devotes 16 hours a day to hard study may become at 60 as wise as he thought himself at 20.

Mary Wilson Little

....

Two forty-somethings are discussing getting enough exercise in middle and old age. 'Well, my mum's a great example,' says one. 'She began walking five miles a days when she was sixty and now she's ninety-three.' 'That's incredible' says his friend. 'Yes, but it's worrying. We don't have a clue where she is.'

....

Wrinkles should merely indicate where smiles have been.

Mark Twain

We are young only once, after that
we need some other excuse.

Anonymous

....

If you don't learn to laugh at trouble,
you won't have anything to laugh
at when you're old.

Edgar Watson Howe

....

Be nice to your kids – they'll be
choosing your nursing home.

Anonymous

In 2005, a study of over 400 pensioners
found that cognitive ability is not a prime
factor in achieving satisfaction in life.
Although being smart is something
that helps you get on well in life,
when it comes to happiness in later
years it's not such a big deal!

An elderly man is asked by his doctor to provide a semen sample for analysis. He's given a jar and told to come back the next day. When the old man returns, the jar is still clean and empty as it was the day before. The doctor asks for an explanation. 'Well, doctor, I tried with my right hand, then my left hand, but it was no good. Then I got my wife to help me. She tried with both hands, then her mouth, first with her teeth in, then her teeth out. We even asked the milkman. He tried with both hands, then under his armpit, and he even tried squeezing it between his knees... but still nothing.' The doctor can't believe what he's hearing. 'You asked the milkman?' 'Yes, doc,' he replies. 'But none of us can get the lid off.'

Growing old is like
being increasingly
penalised for a crime
you haven't committed.

ANTHONY POWELL

Few people know how to be old.

François de la Rochefoucauld

....

Betty is very fond of playing with her granddaughter and asking her about shapes, colours and animals. Whichever question she asks, the girl always gets it right. This goes on for weeks and, eventually growing tired of it all, the young girl says, 'Grandma, don't you think it's time you tried to work some of these out for yourself?'

....

One should never make one's debut in a scandal. One should reserve that to give interest to one's old age.

Oscar Wilde

When you get to 52, food becomes more important than sex.

Prue Leith

....

I wouldn't like to die on stage. I'd settle for room service and a couple of dissipated women.

Peter O'Toole

....

A man is not old until his regrets take the place of dreams.

John Barrymore

The oldest person to receive a Nobel Prize is Leonid Hurwicz, who received the prize for Economics in 2007 at the age of 90. It's never too late to make a difference!

If you young fellows were wise, the devil couldn't do anything to you, but since you aren't wise, you need us who are old.

Martin Luther

....

I'm 59 and people call me middle aged. How many 118-year-old men do you know?

Barry Cryer

....

You know you're getting old when you can pinch an inch on your forehead.

John Mendoza

Three senior citizens who are all worried about their increasing memory loss arrive at the doctors to get themselves tested. The doctor tells them he's going to ask them a series of simple quick-fire questions and they should answer straight away. 'What's three times three?' the doctor asks the first man. 'Two-hundred-and-seventy-four,' the patient shoots back. 'Hmm,' says the doctor. 'I'll come back to you. Now it's your turn,' he says to the second man, 'What is three times three?' 'Tuesday,' he replies.

'That's not right either,' says the doctor. Finally, he asks the third man, 'OK, your turn. What's three times three?' 'Nine,' says the third patient.

'That's great!' the doctor says. 'So how did you know that?' 'Simple,' says the third man. 'I subtracted two-hundred-and-seventy-four from Tuesday.'

LIFE'S LITTLE PLEASURES

If I had my life to live over again, I would make the same mistakes, only sooner.

Tallulah Bankhead

Maybe it's because I'm getting older... the simple act of tasting a glass of wine is its own event.

DAVID HYDE PIERCE

No matter what happens, I'm loud, noisy, earthy and ready for much more living.

Elizabeth Taylor

....

During a meal to celebrate their fiftieth wedding anniversary, Peggy notices her husband, Charlie, welling up. 'Are you getting emotional about our fifty wonderful years together? she asks.
'Oh, no,' he replies, 'I was remembering your dad threatening me on our wedding day and saying he'd have me thrown in jail for fifty years if I didn't marry you. I would've been a free man tomorrow!'

....

Passing the vodka bottle and playing the guitar.

Keith Richards on how he keeps fit

Amy and Evie, two elderly widows, live in a seniors' housing community. Amy is keen to get acquainted with a new neighbour – a very handsome gentleman who keeps himself to himself and seems rather lonely.

Amy says, 'You know I'm shy, Evie. Can you strike up a conversation and find out a bit about him?'

Evie agrees. She spots him walking on his own in the gardens and says hello. 'Excuse me, sir. My friend and I are wondering why you look so lonely.'

'Because I've spent the past thirty years in prison,' he says.

'Oh,' says Evie, taken aback. 'What for?'

'For shooting my third wife.'

'What happened to your second wife?'

'Oh, I strangled her.'

'And, if I may ask, your first wife?'

'She got fatally stabbed during an argument.'

'Goodness,' says Evie, stunned. Then she yells over to her friend, 'Yoo hoo, Amy. He's single!'

I'm like old wine. They don't bring me out very often, but I'm well preserved.

Rose Fitzgerald Kennedy

....

Water, taken in moderation, cannot hurt anybody.

Mark Twain

....

I can still enjoy sex at 74. I live at 75, so it's no distance.

Bob Monkhouse

Fascinating fact

Approaching 100 years of age, John Lowe is Britain's oldest ballet dancer. In his life he has been a soldier in World War Two, an art teacher and a theatre director, but now dedicates his time to dance, to the point of even having installed a trapeze in his living room!

It's important to have a twinkle in your wrinkle.

ANONYMOUS

One of the best parts of growing older? You can flirt all you like since you've become harmless.

Liz Smith

....

A man and his brother-in-law are discussing
the benefits of life as retirees.
'I love the freedom to play golf, have a lunchtime
beer, and generally do what I want,
when I want,' says one.
'I never even know what day of the week it is,'
boasts the other. 'All I know is, the day the big
paper comes, I dress up and go to church.'

....

How people keep correcting us when we are young! There is always some bad habit or other they tell us we ought to get over. Yet most bad habits are tools to help us through life.

Friedrich Nietzsche

Brian had worked at the brewery for over 50 years, but one day he lost his footing on a walkway, fell into a beer vat and drowned. The foreman decided he would break the news of his death to his widow. He arrived at the house and rang the bell. When she answered, he said: 'I'm so sorry to have to tell you Julie, but your poor husband passed away at work today. He must have lost concentration – he fell into the vat and he drowned.'

She was understandably distraught and wept uncontrollably while the foreman did his best to console her. After about 20 minutes she gathered herself. 'Tell me, do you think he suffered in there?'

'Well, knowing Brian as well as I did, I don't think so,' said the foreman. 'He got out three times to go to the loo.'

Give me chastity and continence, but not yet.

Saint Augustine

....

A retired man goes to see the doctor as he's struggling to speak and has a very sore throat. After various tests the doctor tells him he's got laryngitis. She writes him a prescription and asks him to confirm his age to complete the paperwork.

'I'm sixty-two,' he whispers.

'Don't worry,' she whispers back.

'I won't tell anyone.'

....

You are never too old to set another goal or to dream a new dream.

Les Brown

It's sex, not youth, that's wasted on the young.

Janet Harris

. . . .

An old lady heads into a restaurant while her husband parks the car. The waitress shows her to the table and the old lady asks her to keep a watch out for her other half. 'He's got silver hair, a big belly and he wears glasses…' 'Madam,' the waitress interrupts, 'today is pensioners' day. Everyone looks like that.'

. . . .

My doctor told me to watch my drinking, so I now do it in front of the mirror.

Rodney Dangerfield

Four old-time Londoners are having a chat over a
few pints in the pub one lunchtime. After discussing the news,
football, old work colleagues and the good old days,
the conversation eventually turns to their wives.
All four men have had long marriages.
One gentleman turns to the man on his right and asks,
'Steve, aren't you and Doreen celebrating
your fiftieth wedding anniversary soon?'
'Yeah, that's right, we are,' Steve replies.
'So, are you going to do anything special
to celebrate?' another man asks.
Steve ponders this for a few moments. 'Well, I made
quite a big thing of our twenty-fifth anniversary –
I took Doreen to the Scottish Highlands. I suppose
for our fiftieth I could go back and get her.'

*I'm too old to
do things by half.*

LOU REED

The secret to staying young is to live honestly, eat slowly, and lie about your age.

Lucille Ball

....

I don't need drugs any more, thank God. I can get the same effect just by standing up real fast.

Jonathan Katz

....

Most grandmas have a touch of the scallywag.

Helen Thomson

I'd hate to die with a good liver, good kidneys and a good brain... I want everything to be knackered.

Hamish Imlach

....

An old man and his grandson, both big football fans, are watching a match on TV. Grandad starts getting a little wistful. 'You know,' he says, 'It's not easy getting old. I'm seventy-five now and, in football terms, I'm deep into the second half.' 'Oh, don't worry, Grandad,' replies the boy. 'Maybe you'll go into extra time.'

....

If they don't have chocolate in heaven I'm not going.

Roseanne Barr

Wine is a living liquid containing no preservatives.

Julia Child

....

A very old lady, whose time is near, wants to meet her maker on her own terms. After weighing up various methods of ending her life, she resolves to shoot herself through the heart. Keen not to mess it up she phones her doctor who tells her the heart is located two inches below the left nipple. So she finishes the call, takes aim… and shoots herself in the left knee.

....

All decent people live beyond their incomes nowadays, and those who aren't respectable live beyond other peoples'.

Saki

A retired couple head into town and visit the local supermarket.
They're only in there five minutes, and when they come out
there's an overzealous parking warden writing out a ticket. They
go up to him and say, 'Come on, man! What are you doing?'
But the warden ignores them and continues writing.
The old man calls him a fascist. But that just gets the
warden's back up and he writes another ticket for being in the
wrong bay and slaps it on the windscreen alongside the first.
Then the man's wife calls him a 'heartless b***ard.'
This results in a third ticket.
This goes on for about 20 minutes and both parties are getting
furious. Eventually the warden says, 'Look, if you two keep
insulting me then I'm going to keep on issuing fines!'
'That's no skin off my nose,' says the man.
'This isn't our car – we came on the bus.'

Fascinating fact

Dubbed 'grandad-olescents', an increasing number of retirees are choosing to forget about the bank balance and have a ball. A survey in 2008 noted that over a fifth of the 2,000 baby-boomers interviewed planned a long-haul round-the-world trip for their retirement, regardless of financial uncertainty, and a 2017 study found that people between the ages of 60 and 72 travelled most intensively.

The more you praise and celebrate your life, the more there is in life to celebrate.

OPRAH WINFREY

The older one grows, the more one likes indecency.

Virginia Woolf

....

A grandson buys his music-loving
grandad a CD player and CDs for Christmas.
The old man is delighted to discover that
he no longer needs to rewind tapes or
move the needle on his record player.
About a week later the grandson
asks how he's getting on.
'Yes, fine,' says grandad.
'I listened to Elvis Presley this morning.'
'The whole CD?' asks the boy.
'No, just one side.'

....

There's a beauty to wisdom and experience that cannot be faked. It's impossible to be mature without having lived.

Amy Grant

Hatred of domestic work is a natural and admirable result of civilisation.

Rebecca West

....

I've never met a woman in my life who would give up lunch for sex.

Erma Bombeck

....

If you obey all the rules, you miss all the fun.

Katharine Hepburn

The lovely thing about being 40 is that you can appreciate 25-year-old men more.

Colleen McCullough

....

An old-timer can't find a seat on a crowded bus.
As the bus goes round a sharp corner, the old
fellow, unable to support himself properly with
his cane, falls over. A little tearaway sitting nearby
says, 'If you'd put a rubber cap on the end of your
cane, you wouldn't have fallen.'
'If your dad had done the same,' he replies.
'I'd have a place to sit.'

....

When I'm old and grey, I want to have a house by the sea... with a lot of wonderful chums, good music and booze around.

Ava Gardner

Spicing things up in your later years is never out of the question. Just ask Dorothy Dale Kloss, 95, who is the world's oldest performing showgirl. She first performed in the 1930s and apparently taught Bob Fosse to dance.

An old man has lived alone since his son was sent to prison. He wants to dig a patch of earth to plant potatoes but it's gruelling work. He writes to his son. 'Dear Tony, I'm feeling depressed because I won't be able to plant my potatoes this year; I'm just too old to be out there digging. I know you would do it for me if you were here. Love Dad.' A week later he receives a letter back from his son. 'Dear Dad, don't dig up that garden for God's sake, that's where I buried all the BODIES. Love Tony.' At first light the next day the old man is woken by sirens. The police dig up the entire back garden but eventually leave, full of apologies, without finding anything. The next day another letter arrives. 'Dear Dad, you can plant the potatoes now. It's the best I could do in the circumstances. Love, Tony.'

There comes a time in every woman's life when the only thing that helps is a glass of champagne.

BETTE DAVIS

Seize the moment. Remember all
those women on the Titanic
who waved off the dessert cart.

Erma Bombeck

....

Anything worth doing is worth overdoing.

Mick Jagger

....

I'm limitless as far as age is concerned...
as long as he has a driver's licence.

Kim Cattrall on dating younger men

A man is only as old as the woman he feels.

Groucho Marx

....

Mavis and Leila love all forms of knitting
and needlework so they are delighted when a
local museum puts on a display of quilts from
around the world. But when they get there
they are shocked at the admission charge.
'Twenty pounds!' said Mavis to the curator, that's
a bit steep. 'Isn't there a discount for pensioners?'
'Ladies,' she said, 'this is a quilt museum.
We give discounts to teenagers.'

....

With mirth and laughter let old wrinkles come.

William Shakespeare

Fascinating fact

For some, retirement – having the freedom to enjoy each day without the business of a regular occupation – can be daunting. But fear not! A study conducted in 2015 revealed that retirement is likely to improve your overall happiness and health.

Think big thoughts but relish small pleasures.

H. Jackson Brown Jr

....

The aim of life is to live, and to live means to be aware, joyously, drunkenly, serenely, divinely aware.

Henry Miller

....

I finally figured out the only reason to be alive is to enjoy it.

Rita Mae Brown

STILL
GOT IT

Life may not be the party
we hoped for, but while we're
here we should dance.

Proverb

When it comes
to staying young,
a mind-lift beats
a face-lift any day.

MARTY BUCELLA

A little old lady, only 4 feet 8 inches in shoes, decides to get fit, so she heads to her local gym for a free personal training session. Her muscly young instructor bounds up, greets her warmly, shows her to the female changing rooms and says he'll meet her in the exercise area in a few minutes.

A little while later she emerges dressed in her gym kit. The instructor is not there so, noticing a silver bar along one wall that's not in use, she decides to attempt a few chin-ups while she waits. She can barely reach the bar, even with jumping, but eventually gets hold and manages two chin-ups, before she becomes aware of the instructor standing alongside her, looking perplexed.

'OK,' he says, 'if you want to let go of that hand rail and follow me, we can get started.'

A woman stops to speak to an old man who's
sitting in his front garden, smiling away.
'You look so content,' she says.
'What's your secret?'
'I drink a bottle of vodka a day and smoke
sixty cigarettes' he says. 'And I've got a
terrible diet and I never exercise.'
'That's incredible,' the woman says.
'How old are you?'
'Twenty-eight.'

....

There are people whose watch stops at a certain hour and who remain permanently at that age.

Helen Rowland

I could not, at any age, be content to take my place by the fireside and simply look on. Life was meant to be lived.

Eleanor Roosevelt

· ·

Old age is like everything else. To make a success of it, you've got to start young.

Fred Astaire

· ·

I reckon responsible behaviour is something to get when you grow older. Like varicose veins.

Terry Pratchett

Christopher Lee, the actor known for his roles in as Dracula for Hammer Horror and Saruman in The Lord of the Rings trilogy, made his debut as a heavy metal vocalist at the age of 87, with his concept album about King Charlemagne, founder of the Holy Roman Empire.

My heroes are people like Picasso
and Miró and people who at last
really reach something in their old
age, which they absolutely couldn't
ever have done in their old age,
which they absolutely couldn't ever
have done in their youth.

ROBERT WYATT

Bill and Maud, both in their nineties, are making plans for their wedding. Out walking one day they pass a chemist's and go inside. After chatting casually to the pharmacist for a couple of minutes about their nuptials, Bill asks, 'Do you sell heart medication?'

'Of course we do,' the pharmacist replies.

'What about medicine for rheumatism?'

'Sure.'

'How about Viagra?'

'Yes, it's right over here.'

'Pills and potions for memory problems, arthritis, jaundice, gout?'

'Yes, definitely.'

'What about vitamins and sleeping pills?'

'Absolutely.'

'How about wheelchairs and walking frames?'

'Yes, we've got those out the back,' says the pharmacist, growing a little irritated. 'But why do you ask?'

'Well,' says Bill. 'We'd like to register for our wedding gifts here, please.'

I'm saving that rocker for the day when I feel as old as I really am.

Dwight D. Eisenhower

....

An elderly fellow is struggling with his sex life. The medical profession can't help, so he goes to see a faith healer. 'Can you give me an erection?' he asks. 'I'm sorry sir,' says the faith healer. 'I can make a blind man see, make the lame walk and I can even cure cancer – but I can't raise the dead.'

....

Some people are born old and tired while others are going strong at 70.

Dorothy Thompson

Two police officers see an old woman staggering out of a local pub. Stopping to speak to her, it's clear she's had far too much to drink, so they decide to help her out and drive her home. They stick her in the back and one of the officers sits next to her to check she isn't sick. As they drive along, they keep asking her where she lives, but she just keeps lolling over the officer, stroking his arm and saying, 'You're passionate, you're passionate.' This happens about 20 times and the officers are getting rather tired of it all.

'Look,' says the driver, clearly exasperated. 'We have driven you round and round for well over an hour and you still haven't actually told us where you live!'

She says, 'Well, I keep trying to tell you, you're passin' it!'

In the midst of winter, I finally
learned that there was in me
an invincible summer.

Albert Camus

....

We are always the same age inside.

Gertrude Stein

....

You are only young once, but you
can be immature for a lifetime.

John P. Grier

A pair of sixty-something neighbours who like a drink are enjoying a tipple or three in their communal garden.
One turns to the other and confesses to have drunk more than usual the day before.
'What's more than usual?' asks his neighbour.
'A case.'
'What! You can drink a case in a day?!'
'Hang on,' the first man grumbles defensively, 'it doesn't take me all day.'

If you rest, you rust.

Helen Hayes

....

A young granddaughter is staying at her
grandparents' house for the weekend. She is
intrigued by her grandmother's make-up routine,
especially when the old lady takes the lid
off a huge tub of white goo.
'Wow, what are you doing now?' asks the little girl.
'I'm putting on my wrinkle cream,' says the granny.
'Oh,' the girl says, walking away.
'I thought they were natural.'

....

Inside every older person is a younger person – wondering what the hell happened.

Cora Harvey Armstrong

When you are dissatisfied and would like to go back to your youth... think of algebra.

WILL ROGERS

Like many women my age, I am 28 years old.

Mary Schmich

....

Two school reunion events are taking place in the
same hotel – one a 50-year reunion, the other 40.
A group of the older women are having a natter
in the ladies' room when they notice a group of
younger women, unknown to them, staring. It
becomes uncomfortable and one breaks the silence.
'Er, excuse me, what are you looking at?'
'Oh, don't mind us. We just wanted to see how
we'd look in another ten years.'

....

Age should not have its face lifted, but it should rather teach the world to admire wrinkles as the etchings of experience.

Clarence Day

The best tunes are played on the oldest fiddles.

Ralph Waldo Emerson

....

A widow goes to see a grief counsellor to discuss her husband's death. 'We were married thirty years before he died,' she says, drying her eyes. 'And we never had an argument in all that time.' 'That's incredible,' says the counsellor. 'Why do you think that was?' 'Well, I outweighed him by forty pounds and he was a coward.'

An elderly woman goes to her local doctor's surgery. She gets called into the consultation room, takes a seat and the doctor asks her why she's come. 'I'd like to have some birth control pills please, doctor,' she says.

Taken back, the doctor thinks for a minute and says, 'But Mrs. Turpin, you're eighty years old. What would you possibly need birth control pills for?'

'They help me sleep better,' replies the old lady.

The doctor considers this for a moment. 'Well, in all my years of practice I've never heard of that as a side effect. How do birth control pills help you sleep?'

'Oh, I put them in my granddaughter's orange juice when she's not looking,' she explains, 'and I sleep a lot better at night.'

A study in 2015 found that 54 per cent of married men and 31 per cent of married women over 70 were still having sex regularly – still got it and still getting it!

Keep on raging —
to stop the aging.

DALE CARNEGIE

Time and trouble will tame an advanced young woman, but an advanced old woman is uncontrollable by any earthly force.

Dorothy L. Sayers

....

When they tell me I'm too old to do something, I attempt it immediately.

Pablo Picasso

....

When people tell you how young you look they are also telling you how old you are.

Cary Grant

You can't help getting older, but you don't have to get old.

George Burns

. . . .

The queen is being given a tour of a nursing home
as part of her royal duties. The queen passes a little
old man who seems to look right through her
as he shuffles past. She steps back and asks,
'Excuse me, do you know who I am?'
The old man looks up and points back to the front
desk. 'No, but if you go down there they'll tell you.'

. . . .

Fifty is the new thirty-four.

Emma Soames

British pilot David Marks broke the world record for the oldest person to make a solo helicopter flight in 2017 when he flew between Northampton Sywell Airfield and Fenland Airfield at the age of 87.

You're never too old
to become younger.

MAE WEST

A young staff member is talking to a nursing home resident. It turns out that many years ago the old man travelled the world as an intrepid explorer.
'What's the most terrifying experience you've ever had?' asks the young nurse.
'Oh, once I was tracking Bengal tigers in the jungles of India,' he begins. 'I was walking a very narrow path and all of a sudden, there in front of me was the biggest tiger I ever saw. I tried to get my weapon ready, but there was no time, the tiger leapt towards me and gave a mighty roooaarrrrr! I soiled myself.'
'That sounds really frightening,' says the nurse. 'Given those circumstances I think anybody would have done the same.'
'Oh, no not then,' replies the old explorer. 'Just now when I went roooaarrrrr!'

The ageing process has you firmly in
its grasp if you never get the urge
to throw a snowball.

Doug Larson

....

I'm surprised that I'm 50...
I still feel like a kid.

Bruce Willis

....

It's too late for me to retire now.

Michael Caine at 70

We are happier in many ways when we are old than when we were young. The young sow wild oats. The old grow sage.

WINSTON CHURCHILL

Another belief of mine: that everyone else my age is an adult, whereas I am merely in disguise.

Margaret Atwood

....

A pair of old widows, Aisha and Doris, are getting back into the dating game. When they meet up one Monday morning, Doris is eager to know how Aisha's Saturday night blind date went.
'Oh, it was awful,' says Aisha. 'He showed up in a nineteen-twenties Rolls-Royce.'
'But what's so terrible about that?' says Doris, sounding jealous.
'He was the original owner.'

....

There is no pleasure worth forgoing just for an extra three years in the geriatric ward.

John Mortimer

A study from 2016 found that people over the age of 65 are more confident when dating – they know what they're looking for and are better at quickly working out whether they fancy someone or not, with the majority calling time on a date in less than an hour if they're not interested. On the plus side, it also means that love at first sight happens more often in later life, with one in four over-65s confidently able to say whether they are attracted to someone within seconds.

Getting old ain't for sissies.

Bette Davis

....

It is not by the grey of the hair that one knows the age of the heart.

Edward G. Bulwer-Lytton

....

The older you get the more important it is not to act your age.

Ashleigh Brilliant

Tracey is chatting to some friends in a bar. She's had cancer several times – including a double mastectomy and reconstructive surgery – but she's always the life and soul of the party. When her old friend John comes in, they hug warmly and John notices something is missing.

'Tracey, you're not wearing a bra!' he whispers.

'Well, I may be seventy,' she says, 'but they're only seventeen.'

Don't let ageing get you
down. It's too hard
to get back up.

JOHN WAGNER

Suddenly SENIOR

THE FUNNY THING ABOUT GETTING OLDER

TOM HAY

SUDDENLY SENIOR

Tom Hay

ISBN: 978 1 84953 920 3

£9.99

Hardback

You might be getting a bit thin on top, plump
at the middle and creaky around the knees, but
that doesn't mean you've forgotten how to enjoy
yourself! This collection of witty quotations, light-
hearted yarns and cheerful jokes will help you chalk
that last senior moment down to experience, forget
the grey hairs and the twinges, and celebrate
getting older with a smile on your face and

A TWINKLE IN YOUR WRINKLE.

If you're interested in finding out more about our books,
find us on Facebook at **Summersdale Publishers** and
follow us on Twitter at **@Summersdale**.

www.summersdale.com